the cat care book

the cat care book

A Quick-Start Guide for New Cat Owners

carolyn kaye

Copyright © 2025 by Carolyn Kaye

All rights reserved.

No part of this book may be reproduced in any form or by any electronic or mechanical means, including information storage and retrieval systems, without written permission from the author, except for the use of brief quotations in a book review.

NO AI TRAINING: Without in any way limiting the author's [and publisher's] exclusive rights under copyright, any use of this publication to "train" generative artificial intelligence (AI) technologies to generate text or images is expressly prohibited. The author reserves all rights to license uses of this work for generative AI training and development of machine learning language models.

First edition

Paperback ISBN: 979-8-218-88565-6

Hardcover ISBN: 979-8-218-91961-0

Published in the United States of America

Disclaimer:

The information provided in this book is for general informational purposes only. While the author has made every effort to ensure the accuracy of the information, this book is not intended to provide veterinary advice. Readers are encouraged to seek professional consultation for advice specific to their individual circumstances. The author assumes no responsibility for errors or omissions, or for any damages that may result from the use of the information contained herein.

Brand names mentioned in this book are property of their respective owners. The publisher of this book is not affiliated with any organizations mentioned in this book. This book has not been endorsed by any organizations mentioned in this book.

contents

Introduction — vii
1. Cat Supplies — 1
2. Feed Your Cat a Healthy Food — 3
3. Choose Suitable Food and Water Bowls — 9
4. Have a Litter Box and Accessories — 11
5. Brush Your Cat — 17
6. Bathe Your Cat (But Not Too Often) — 21
7. Keep Your Cat's Claws Trimmed — 23
8. Brush Your Cat's Teeth — 27
9. Enjoy Playtime — 29
10. Buy a Scratching Post or Scratcher — 35
11. Provide a Napping Spot — 41
12. Have Treats — 43
13. Invest in a Good Cat Carrier — 47
14. Find a Good Veterinarian — 51
15. Make Your Home Cat-Safe — 55
16. If You Have a Dog, Introduce Your Pets Slowly — 63
17. Teach Children How to Treat Your Cat — 65
18. Keep Your Cat Indoors — 67

Closing — 69
About the Author — 71

introduction

Getting a cat or kitten is an exciting time in one's life. As you may already know or will soon find out, cats are so many things: fun, playful, independent, loving, curious, intelligent, and often very entertaining. Since you got this book about cat care, your pet is lucky to have a caring owner.

As a cat lover and long-time cat owner, I wrote this book to teach first-time cat owners the need-to-know essentials of caring for a cat. I've also included many tips and tricks I've learned to keep cats happy and healthy.

Preparing for Your New Cat

Before bringing your cat home, you'll need to have a litter box ready, food and water bowls, food, a cat bed or blanket, and a scratching post. You'll find a supply list in Chapter 1 and information throughout this book to help you choose the right items for your cat.

Once you have the basic supplies, it's time to look around your home for potential hazards to your cat. From toxic plants to electrical cords and more, Chapter 15 covers common dangers and offers tips to create a cat-friendly environment.

If you have a dog, it's best to set up a temporary, separate room for your cat to give them time to get settled in their new home before they meet your dog. Chapter 16 provides tips for introducing a cat and dog slowly so they can develop a positive relationship and lifelong friendship.

Your Cat's First Days at Home

Your cat's first days at home are a special time for you and your cat. To help him or her become acclimated to their new surroundings, give them time to explore at their own pace. Show them where to find their food, water, litter box, toys, and bed. Put a scratching post in an area where they spend the most time. Cats appreciate a calm and peaceful environment during this period.

Depending on their personality, some cats adapt to new environments quickly, while others are more timid or may hide until they feel safe. Don't take this personally; it's a normal, self-protective instinct. If your cat hides, place their food and water bowls in a location they can see and speak calmly to them so they become familiar with your voice. Eventually, your cat will feel comfortable enough to come out of hiding.

Cats thrive on routine, so keeping a regular meal schedule will be comforting to them. In their first few weeks as part of your family, let your cat set the pace of how much they want to socialize, rest, or play. Your patience will be rewarded as you earn the trust and love of your cat.

1
cat supplies

Here is a list of supplies you'll need for your new friend. I suggest having the items on the 'Essentials' list ready when you bring your cat home.

Essentials

- Canned or Dry Cat Food
- Food Dish
- Water Bowls
- Litter Box
- Litter
- Litter Scoop & Bucket
- Bed or Blanket
- Scratcher or Scratching Posts
- Cat Toys
- Cat Carrier

Care & Cleaning

- Brush
- Cat Nail Scissors
- Pet Styptic Powder
- Cat Shampoo
- Cat Dental Care Kit
- Cat First Aid Kit
- Enzyme Cleaner for Cat Urine
- Towels

Other

- Cat Treats
- Bag of Pure, Dried Catnip
- Organic Cat Grass
- Litter Mat

2
feed your cat a healthy food

SELECTING A CAT FOOD IS ONE OF THE MOST IMPORTANT decisions you will make as a cat owner. The right food can help keep your cat healthy, energetic, and at a proper weight throughout its life. It should also be a food your cat enjoys and one you feel good about feeding him or her. Here are several factors to consider when choosing cat food.

Your Cat's Age

- **Kittens:** Cats under a year old should eat kitten food unless your vet tells you to switch to an adult formula. Kittens grow fast and need food with extra calories.
- **Adult Cats:** Cats between one and seven years old should eat an adult formula.
- **Senior Cats:** Cats seven or older should eat a senior formula.

Your Cat's Activity Level

Consider how active your cat is to ensure he or she gets enough (and not too many) calories. If you have an active, healthy cat at a normal weight, a regular adult formula would be the best choice.

For less active cats that are kept indoors, or those that gain too much weight with regular adult cat food, consider an indoor formula. Indoor formulas typically have a lower fat content, which can help prevent weight gain.

Ingredients

Cat foods vary widely in nutrition and quality, so it's helpful to read the label of foods you're considering. The first three to five ingredients listed on the label matter most because they comprise the largest percentage of the food. Since cats are carnivores, quality cat food will contain real meat or meat meal within the first few ingredients.

The following are some basics to remember when reading a cat food label. These are just general guidelines. Cat foods don't have to have everything on the "good" list to be good quality food.

Good for Your Cat

- Real meats or meat meals in the first three listed ingredients
- Foods that don't contain by-products
- Foods without added artificial flavors, colors, or artificial preservatives
- Rice
- Eggs
- Natural fat sources, like sunflower or fish oils
- Fiber from plant sources
- Added vitamins and minerals like taurine, vitamin A, linoleic acid
- Foods with meats and other ingredients made in your own country
- Tocopherol—this is vitamin E used as a natural preservative

What to Avoid

- Foods without real meat or meat meal in the first three ingredients
- Corn or corn gluten meal (it's an inexpensive filler that many cats don't do well on)
- Wheat (for the same reason as corn)
- By-products (these could be beaks, feet, and even feathers)
- Artificial colors, flavors, or preservatives like BHT, BHA, or Ethoxyquin

- Beef tallow

Your Budget

Better quality cat food generally costs more because higher quality meats, natural ingredients, and natural preservatives (like vitamin E) are more expensive. These foods also contain fewer fillers, so a can or bag of a healthy cat food will provide your cat with more nutritional value than the same quantity of a food filled with corn, wheat, by-products, and artificial colors and flavors.

Make a habit of reading ingredient labels, and purchase the best quality food you can afford. In my experience, paying a little more for better quality food helps prevent potential issues caused by poor quality food, like allergies, digestive problems, vomiting, loose stool, dull coat, or low energy.

Your Cat's Health

If your cat is overweight or has a health issue, your veterinarian may suggest a special food or diet for their condition.

General Cat Food Tips

- Cats should eat cat food to be healthy. Dog food or even a can of tuna won't provide complete nutrition.
- If you know what food your cat was eating before bringing them home, get a small amount of the same food to keep them on a consistent diet and gradually transition to the food you plan on feeding them to help prevent stomach upset.
- When switching cat food brands, mix a small amount of the new food into your cat's current food, reducing

the amount of old food each day to make the change easier for your cat's digestion.
- Monitor how your cat is doing on the new food. Over time, you may need to transition to another food as their age, weight, activity level, or health changes.
- Some cats will eat every food they're offered, and others have specific flavor preferences like seafood, chicken, or beef. If your cat is a picky eater, buy a variety of flavors to find which ones they enjoy the most.

Should You Buy Canned or Dry Cat Food?

Feeding canned or dry food is a personal choice. Dry food is convenient for busy people because it can sit out all day without the risk of spoiling. Canned food gives cats additional hydration, which is beneficial to their health. Many people like to feed a combination of canned and dry.

> **Safety Tip:** Canned cat food shouldn't be left out more than a half-hour (20 minutes in hot weather) because it can spoil and become unsafe to eat. Cover and refrigerate leftover food in the can and dispose of uneaten food in the bowl.

How Much Food Should I Feed My Cat?

The amount of food to feed your cat will depend on their weight and activity level. It's best to follow the suggested amount listed on the specific food you're feeding them or ask your veterinarian for guidance.

If you feed them dry and canned food, consider that when determining the best amount.

If your cat is gaining too much weight, ask your veterinarian for suggestions. They may gradually reduce the portion size or suggest you feed them a reduced calorie or indoor formula.

3
choose suitable food and water bowls

Stainless steel or ceramic dishes are the best options for your cat's food and water. Unlike plastic, these materials don't retain odors and are easy to clean. It's helpful to have several dishes and bowls, so you always have a clean one ready to use.

. . .

Food Dishes

Opt for shallow food dishes, as they are easier for cats to eat from. Look for dishes with rubber on the base to prevent them from sliding while your cat eats. Or, place the dish on a small rubber mat for added stability.

Water Bowls

Have a bowl of water available at all times for your cat. Cats prefer fresh water, so it's important to change the water at least once a day and wash the bowl with warm water and mild dish soap a few times a week.

> **Tip:** It's essential to keep your cat hydrated throughout the day. To encourage more water consumption, consider placing water bowls in two locations.

4
have a litter box and accessories

A LITTER BOX, LITTER, AND A SCOOP ARE NECESSITIES FOR EVERY cat owner. Here are the basics to know about litter boxes and how to keep them clean.

Litter Box

There are many varieties of boxes to choose from, from inexpensive plastic boxes to fancy self-cleaning ones. A basic plastic box is the easiest to start with. Many cats prefer this style because it doesn't trap odors or make them feel confined. Whatever type of box you choose, make sure it's large enough. Small boxes are fine for kittens, but cats over ten pounds (4.5 kg) may find a regular box too small. Choose an extra-large one if needed.

> **Tip:** The basic rule of thumb for litter boxes is "one per cat, plus one extra." Yes, it's a little extra work to maintain

multiple boxes, but each one stays clean longer than if you only have one.

Litter

If you're unsure what kind to choose, start with a basic clay litter. It's usually the least expensive, and most cats and kittens are used to it. Look for 'low dust' or 'no dust' varieties because dust is unpleasant for you and your pet.

> **Tip:** Once you find a type and brand of litter that works, stick with it. Switching types too often might cause finicky cats to avoid the box. If you need to switch to something else, transition to the new litter over several days, mixing the old and new litters until your cat adjusts.

Optional: Litter Mat

If you keep a mat under the box, it'll help catch litter before it gets tracked around the house.

Where to Keep the Litter Box

Here's what makes a good place to keep the box:

- A quiet location away from heavy traffic areas and doorways
- Away from the area where the cat eats and drinks
- A room the cat has access to 24/7
- A room where the cat can have some privacy and use the box without interruptions

Litter Scoop and Bucket

Choose a litter scoop that works with the type of litter you buy and a small bucket to dispose of the dirty litter as you scoop.

Scooping the Box

Scoop once or twice daily to keep the box clean and minimize odors. As you scoop, check for anything unusual in their stool or urine (such as worms, mucus, or blood). Also, notice if there is diarrhea, hard stools, or more or less stool than usual. If you see anything that seems abnormal, call your vet to ask about it.

Dump the scooped litter into a garbage bag or dispose of it in a covered trash container to keep odors away from the litter box area.

About once a week, replace all the litter and wash the box with dish detergent and warm water.

> **Tip:** Cats are tidy creatures. If their litter box is dirty, some cats will go to the bathroom someplace else in the home. Keeping the box clean is the best way to prevent this problem.

Weekly Litter Box Cleaning

A weekly cleaning will keep the litter box as clean and odor-free as possible. I've found it helpful to set out a backup box in case the cat needs to use the bathroom before the cleaning is done. It's easiest to clean the box outdoors, but if that's not possible, a wash tub is another option.

Supplies Needed

- A pair of rubber gloves
- A place to dispose of old litter
- A litter scoop/bucket
- Mild dish detergent
- White vinegar
- Old towels or paper towels for clean-up
- Fresh litter

Litter Box Cleaning Steps

1. Dump out all old litter. Use a scoop to scrape any stuck to the sides or bottom.
2. Wash the entire box with a mild dish detergent and warm water. Don't use bleach, ammonia, or any other harsh chemicals that are harmful to cats.
3. Rinse the box completely.
4. If there are still odors after washing, swish a 50/50 white vinegar and water mixture inside the box to help neutralize the smell. Be sure to rinse until there's no vinegar scent in the box. If there are still cat odors in the box after this process, it's time for a replacement.
5. Dry the box completely before adding fresh litter.

How to Clean Areas Soiled With Cat Urine or Feces

If your cat happens to go to the bathroom somewhere other than its litter box, clean the mess by absorbing the urine with paper towels and/or picking up the feces. Then, thoroughly clean the area with an enzyme cleaner for cat urine or a multi-purpose enzyme cleaner for cat urine and feces. A good cleaning and complete rinsing of the soiled area will keep your home smelling fresh and reduce the likelihood that the cat will relieve itself in that location again.

5
brush your cat

BRUSHING YOUR CAT IS EASY AND TAKES ONLY A MINIMAL amount of time. Most cats enjoy being brushed, as it helps them relax. Regular brushing removes dead hair, dander, and dirt while keeping the skin healthy. It also gives you time to bond with your cat.

How Often Should I Brush My Cat?

If your cat has short hair, brush them once a week. Medium or long-haired cats or those with thick, fluffy coats need brushing at least two to three times a week.

Type of Brush

A boar bristle brush works well for most cats. Choose one with firm enough bristles to remove excess hair and leave your cat's coat smooth and tangle-free.

Boar bristle cat brush

If your cat has medium or long hair or sheds a lot, consider using a slicker brush in addition to a bristle brush. The metal bristles of a slicker brush are very effective at removing tangles and preventing mats.

How to Prevent Mats

Mats are hard clumps of fur that form when a cat's coat isn't brushed often enough. Shedding typically increases as the weather warms up, so regular brushing is crucial for removing dead hair and preventing mats.

Mats can develop on cats of any hair type but are more common in medium and long-haired breeds. Once mats form, they can be difficult to remove. If the mats are severe, you may need a professional groomer or veterinarian to shave them off. To prevent this issue, brush your cat regularly.

Brushing Tips:

- Start a brushing routine from the beginning.
- Brush your cat in a quiet location so they're more likely to stay calm and still.

- As you brush, check your cat's coat and skin for any signs of fleas, ticks, rashes, or lumps. If you notice any of these issues, ask your veterinarian.
- Reward him or her with a treat afterward.

6
bathe your cat (but not too often)

Most cats are excellent at grooming themselves. Unless they're dirty from the outdoors or are older and having difficulty cleaning themselves, one or two baths a year is usually sufficient.

Tips for Bathing Your Cat

- Give your cat a thorough brushing before bathing to remove excess hair, knots, tangles, or mats.
- Bathe your cat in a wash tub or bathtub using comfortably warm water.
- Consider using a bath hose for easier rinsing.
- Use a gentle shampoo specifically designed for cats and be careful not to get any soap or water near their eyes or ears.
- Avoid shampoos that contain flea treatments unless recommended by your veterinarian, as some cats may have adverse reactions to these products.

- After the bath, thoroughly dry your cat with a towel and keep her in a warm location until she's dry. Then, give her a good brushing to make her fluffy and beautiful.

7
keep your cat's claws trimmed

YOU'LL NEED A SMALL PAIR OF CAT SCISSORS TO TRIM YOUR CAT'S claws. Regular trimming will prevent them from becoming too long, sharp, broken, or frayed. Long claws can lead to accidental scratches when you're holding your cat, or they can snag on clothing, carpet, and furniture.

It's usually sufficient to trim claws once or twice a month. Typically, the front claws grow faster than the back ones. Make sure your scissors are sharp, as dull ones will tear the claw instead of cutting it, which can be painful for your cat.

> **Safety Tip:** If you've never trimmed a cat's claws before, have an experienced cat owner, a professional groomer, or a veterinarian show you the proper technique until you feel comfortable doing it on your own.

Steps:

1. Choose a well-lit or sunny room.
2. Have someone hold the cat still, or do it yourself if you can.
3. Place your pet on a table, your lap, or the floor—whatever works best for you.
4. For the front paws, gently press on one toe to extend the claw.
5. Locate the 'quick,' which is the pinkish vein that extends down through the nail.
6. Trim only the tip of the claw and be very careful not to get close to the quick.
7. Repeat this process for each toe, including the dew claws, which are on the inner part of their front legs near the wrist.

Keep a container of pet styptic powder nearby in case you accidentally cut the quick. If this happens, apply styptic powder to the nail and apply some pressure with a clean towel or paper towel until the bleeding stops. As long as you are cautious and avoid the quick, this should not occur.

Be sure to offer plenty of praise and a few treats after each claw-trimming session to make the experience positive for your cat.

8
brush your cat's teeth

Brushing your cat's teeth may seem unusual, but it's an important habit to adopt to prevent health issues related to poor dental hygiene. Unhealthy teeth, plaque buildup, and gingivitis can lead to bacteria entering the bloodstream and harming major organs such as the liver, kidneys, and heart. By starting a teeth-brushing routine early, it's possible to prevent these problems.

To get started, you'll need a cat dental care kit, which you can find at a pet store or veterinarian's office. These kits usually include a rubber finger brush that looks like a thimble, a small toothbrush, and enzymatic toothpaste specifically designed for cats. It might take some time for both you and your cat to get accustomed to the teeth-brushing process, but with practice, it will become easier.

> **Tip:** Never use human toothpaste on your cat, as it is unsafe. Always use toothpaste specially made for felines.

How Often Should I Brush My Cat's Teeth?

It's ideal to brush your cat's teeth daily, but even two or three teeth brushing sessions per week can improve your pet's dental health.

9
enjoy playtime

CATS AND KITTENS LOVE TO PLAY, SO IT'S A GOOD IDEA TO HAVE a variety of toys to keep them entertained. Cats can have specific toy preferences, so if they show little interest in one type, keep trying until you find something they enjoy. For example, one of my cats loves toy mice he can carry around in his mouth. He even plays fetch like a dog when I toss his favorite toy! My other cat is more entertained by colorful spring toys, which he enjoys batting across the floor until he wears himself out.

Besides being enjoyable, playtime helps cats burn calories. This is especially important for indoor felines, who become less active as they age. Here are a few toys to consider:

Cat Toy Pillows

Cats have endless fun playing with these small, fluffy pillows with crinkle paper and catnip inside. They'll start playing with them independently, or you can toss one across the floor for your cat to chase and wrestle with.

Cat Springs

Plastic cat spring toys are a simple way to get bored, lazy cats moving. Felines love batting them around and chasing them across the floor. This type of toy works best in rooms with hard floors.

Cat Crinkle Balls

Sparkly mylar crinkle balls are an inexpensive yet fun toy option for cats. They are light enough for cats to bat around the floor, and they enjoy the crinkling noise they make.

Cat Tunnels

Collapsible tunnel tubes are available in many shapes and sizes. They're especially fun for kittens, younger cats, or multiple cats to play together. Cats can entertain themselves for hours by hiding, playing, and crawling in and out of the tubes. Consider adding crinkle balls or placing catnip inside the tubes for extra fun.

Wand Toy with Feathers

This interactive cat toy has clip-on feathers attached to a string and wand. You can wave it around to mimic a bird in flight or drag the feathers along the floor to activate your cat's hunting instinct. Even cats that don't respond to other toys will bat, chase, and pounce on the feathers. Because string and feathers could be a choking hazard, keep this toy in a place your cat can't access when you're not playing.

• • •

Cat Scratching Pad with Cat Toy Ball Track

If you're looking for a toy your cat can enjoy even when you're not home, consider this unique circular toy featuring a round track with a toy ball a cat can bat around and a corrugated cardboard center that serves as a scratcher. Sprinkle some catnip on the center to entice him to scratch and play.

My cat loves pushing the ball around the track of this multi-purpose toy.

Catnip Cat Toys

These soft, catnip-infused toys come in assorted shapes and sizes. Cats love to chew on them, bat them around, or even carry them like a mouse.

Cat Toy Variety Pack

If your cat isn't responding to the toys you have, try a variety pack with an assortment of toys for him or her to choose from.

10
buy a scratching post or scratcher

CATS NEED A PLACE TO SCRATCH TO STRETCH THEIR BACK, LEGS, and feet and to keep their claws sharp and healthy. Some cats also scratch to mark their territory, as they have scent glands on their paw pads. Placing several scratching options around

YOUR HOME CAN HELP PREVENT YOUR CAT FROM CLAWING YOUR furniture, carpet, or other inappropriate places.

Types of Cat Scratchers

- **Sisal:** This natural surface has a roughness that some cats like. Many scratching posts or cat trees have sisal rope wrapped around the post.
- **Cardboard:** Cardboard cat scratchers are available in various sizes and shapes. Some are constructed from corrugated cardboard, while others feature a smoother finish that resembles wood.
- **Wood:** Scratching posts made with wood are less common, but many cats prefer the natural feel of wood or tree bark.
- **Carpet:** Scratching posts covered with carpet can work well for some cats, but they might make your cat think it's acceptable to scratch your carpeting, too.
- **Mixed Surface:** Some scratching posts or cat trees have multiple surfaces, such as sisal, carpet, and wood, which gives your cat options.
- **Cat Trees:** These are much bigger than a typical scratching post and provide cats with a place to climb, play, scratch, stretch, and rest. They give your cat its own space to enjoy rather than going near your furniture. If you decide to get one, ensure it's sturdy and stable so it won't tip over when your cat is climbing or scratching.
- **Horizontal Shape:** Horizontal cat scratchers lie flat on the floor so the cat can stand on them and scratch.
- **Vertical Shape:** This type of scratcher stands upright, allowing your cat to reach up and stretch while

scratching. When choosing this style, be sure it's tall enough for your cat to stretch fully and stable enough that it won't tip over during use.

Discover Your Cat's Scratching Preference

It may take some experimentation to see what surfaces and shape scratchers your cat is most attracted to. Notice how your cat scratches. Does she reach up high? If so, a vertical scratcher may be best. If she scratches along the base of the furniture or on the floor, she may prefer a horizontal one. It's worth trying a few styles to find one your cat loves.

Ways to Get Your Cat to Use Their Scratcher

Catnip - Get a small bag of pure, dried catnip and sprinkle or rub it onto your cat's scratcher or post to entice him to scratch there.

The Right Placement - To help redirect his attention, place the scratcher or post near any furniture he tends to scratch. You can also position it near the entrance of a room he frequently visits. If your cat sees the scratcher as he walks in, he may use it and leave your furniture alone.

Put a Cat Scratcher in More Than One Area - I've found that placing cat scratchers in several rooms works wonders for discouraging destructive scratching. You can also buy a few inexpensive scratchers to hang on doorknobs. Cats love finding a place to scratch in an unexpected spot.

Praise - When your cat uses its scratching post, praise them.

Use Treats - To encourage your cat to use its scratcher or post, give a treat as a reward anytime he uses it. While you won't need to continue this practice indefinitely, using treats as a reward initially can help reinforce positive behavior.

A corrugated cardboard scratching ramp

Additional Ways to Stop a Cat From Scratching in the Wrong Place

If your cat continues to scratch your furniture or other inappropriate spots after trying the ideas listed here, here are a few other strategies to consider:

- Immediately clap loudly or give him a firm "no" to stop the behavior.

- Make a hissing sound using a can of compressed air (the type used for cleaning keyboards). Avoid pointing the can at or near the cat; only use it to make a sound to stop the scratching.

- Cover inappropriate places where your cat is scratching with cat scratch deterrent tape.

- If your cat is damaging valuable items, you might need to remove the items or cover them with plastic covers, especially at night or when you're not home. You may not have to do this once your cat is trained to use its scratching post.

- Try spraying perfume on a cotton pad and wiping the places where the cat has been scratching. Cats dislike the scent of perfume, so it might be enough to deter them. Test the surface first to ensure the perfume won't damage or stain your couch or other furniture.

What Not to Do If Your Cat Is Scratching Items in Your Home

- Don't yell at your cat. Not only will it not help, but you'll end up with a cat that's afraid of you.

- Please don't consider de-clawing your cat to solve this problem. If you research the de-clawing procedure, you'll understand why you would never want to subject your beloved feline friend to something so horrible.

Patience, Consistency, and Praise = Success

Redirecting scratching to appropriate places may take time and patience, but consistent effort, ample praise, and continual reinforcement can lead to success.

11
provide a napping spot

CATS NAP A LOT DURING THE DAY, SO IT'S IMPORTANT TO PROVIDE them with a soft blanket or cozy cat bed. If you live in a cold climate or your home has drafts, a partially enclosed cat bed is best to keep your cat warm. In warmer climates, an open bed is a better option.

Cleaning

All cats love fresh bedding, so wash their blanket or bed liner occasionally to keep it clean and odor-free. If the liner isn't washable, consider placing a soft towel on the bed.

Select the Right Location

Some cats enjoy sleeping in sunny, warm spots, while others prefer to find a dark and private place. Pay attention to where your cat sleeps the most and place the bed in that area.

12
have treats

Our furry friends love treats just as much as we do. Here's what to know about choosing and giving your cat the occasional treat.

Quality

Just like cat food, the quality and nutrition of cat treats varies from brand to brand. When choosing treats, look for ones with quality ingredients, real meat, and little to no fillers. It's also ideal to avoid treats with artificial colors or flavors. I try to give my cats small treats because some larger ones could pose a choking hazard.

Flavors

Cat treats are available in many flavors, including seafood, poultry, beef, greens, and catnip. Each cat has its own flavor preferences, so try a few varieties to see which yours craves most.

How Many to Give

I suggest limiting treats to two or three per day, at most. Eating too many treats may cause stomach issues, weight gain, or make a cat less likely to eat their regular food.

> **Tip:** Keep cat treats secure to prevent your cat from accessing them. Determined cats can open containers and eat all the treats at once!

Organic cat grass

Organic Cat Grass

Many cats enjoy fresh cat grass. You can buy it at certain pet or health food stores or purchase a kit to grow it yourself. It takes just a few days to sprout, and it's entertaining to watch your pet enjoy it.

Catnip

Pure, dried catnip is available in containers or bags. Some pet or health food stores also offer freshly grown organic catnip.

Not all cats react to this herb, but those that do may exhibit unusual behavior. Some will roll around in it, while others may seem more drowsy or playful than usual.

> **Tip:** Catnip can cause some cats to become aggressive or instigate fights with other cats. Therefore, exercise caution until you know how your pet reacts to it.

13
invest in a good cat carrier

A CAT CARRIER IS ESSENTIAL FOR VETERINARY VISITS, TRAVEL, OR in case you need to leave your home during an emergency. Here are some suggestions and tips to help you choose the right type and size of carrier for your feline friend.

. . .

Cat Carrier Basics - What to Look For

- Ensure the carrier has plenty of ventilation.
- The carrier should be roomy enough for your cat to fit comfortably.
- Look for durable construction and secure closures.
- Choose a carrier that's comfortable for you to carry.

Sizing Tips

- Knowing your cat's weight and measurements will help you select the proper size carrier.
- Ensure there is enough room for your cat to turn around, even if he or she can't fully stand up.
- For large cats, a dog carrier might be a better option.
- If you plan to take your cat on a long road trip, a slightly roomier carrier is better so they can occasionally stand up and stretch their legs.
- If you have a kitten, you can buy a small carrier now and a larger one later or purchase one he or she can grow into.

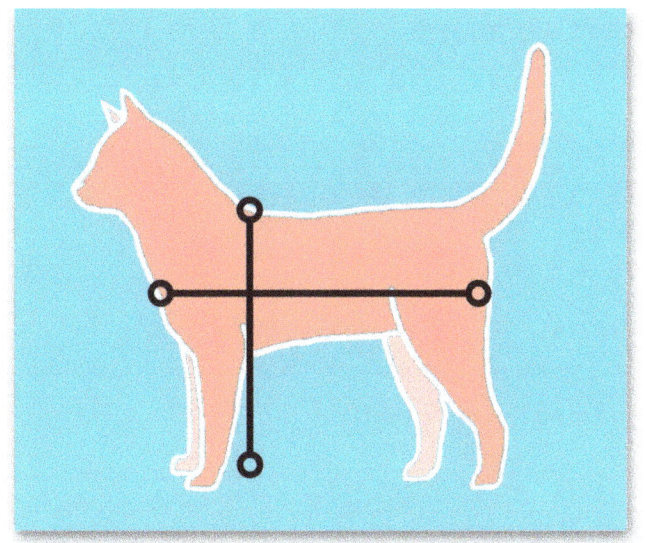

Measure a cat's length from the front of its chest to its rear and height from the top of its back to the floor.

Should You Buy a Soft or Hard Cat Carrier?

Here are some considerations to help you decide between soft and hard carriers:

Hard-Sided Cat Carriers

Pros:

- Easy to clean and sanitize if your cat has an accident.
- Suitable for cats that dislike being in a carrier and may try to claw or chew their way out.

Cons:

- Heavier and not as easy to carry as soft-sided carriers.

Soft-Sided Cat Carriers

Pros:

- Lightweight and easy to carry
- They provide a cozier feel for the cat.
- A good choice for in-cabin air travel, as long as you choose one that fits under the seat
- Most can be spot-cleaned or have a floor liner that can be washed or replaced if needed.

Cons:

- Soft carriers aren't advisable for aggressive cats because some might claw or chew through mesh or fabric.

General Tips

- If you have a strong cat, opt for a hard-sided carrier.
- Cat carriers with front and top openings make it easier to get the cat in and out.
- Inspect the carrier before each use for rips, tears, or broken parts. Verify that all doors, zippers, openings, and latches work to avoid escapes.
- If you plan to travel with your cat by air, ensure the carrier is airline-approved and meets the size requirements to fit beneath your seat. Check with your specific airline for details.

14
find a good veterinarian

If you don't have a veterinarian for other pets, ask friends and family for recommendations of good ones in your area. It's helpful to meet the vet first to ensure they have the proper credentials, are competent and knowledgeable, and charge reasonable fees. Also, try to find someone near your home for easier access in case of an emergency.

The veterinarian will advise you on how often your cat or kitten should have check-ups and vaccinations. They also may talk about spaying or neutering your cat or kitten if this hasn't already been done. Bring a list of questions about your cat's health, diet, or other issues.

A good vet is a valuable ally in keeping your new friend healthy. With proper care, cats can live long, healthy lives.

> **Tip:** Keep your veterinarian's phone number saved on your phone or in an easily accessible location for emergencies.

Signs a Cat Needs Veterinary Attention

Cats are usually very good at hiding signs of illness and injury, so it's up to you to notice changes in their eating, drinking, litter box habits, personality, or day-to-day behavior. The list below provides some signs and symptoms that a cat needs medical attention.

- Going to the bathroom in places other than the litter box
- Blood in urine or stool
- Diarrhea or vomiting
- Changes in their eating habits, such as eating more or less food
- Not eating or drinking
- Changes in weight
- Sleeping more or less than usual
- Less grooming than usual
- Restlessness, agitation, or looking uncomfortable
- Lethargy or weakness
- Sneezing, coughing, wheezing, or difficulty breathing
- Nasal, eye, or ear discharge
- Bad ear odor
- A different appearance to eyes
- Any unusual lumps
- Limping or other signs of pain
- Any signs of fleas or ticks
- Unusual aggression or sudden change in personality
- More vocal than usual
- Shaking head

If your cat shows any of the symptoms mentioned here or has other concerning symptoms or behaviors, please contact your veterinarian.

15
make your home cat-safe

CATS ARE CURIOUS AND LOVE EXPLORING EVERY CORNER OF THEIR homes. This chapter covers potential hazards that could harm your pet's health and well-being. As a new cat owner, taking time to "cat-proof" your living spaces is the best way to

PREVENT ACCIDENTS, ILLNESS, AND INJURIES. HERE ARE A FEW common dangers to be aware of:

- High balconies, ledges, or other high places they can fall from
- Windows without screens
- Glass objects (such as vases) that they can knock down and break
- Lit candles
- Sharp knives or kitchen appliances with sharp blades, like food processors or blenders
- Items they could choke on or swallow like string, dental floss, twist ties, rubber bands, paper clips, safety pins, sewing needles or pins, tiny cat toys
- Medications or pills dropped or spilled onto the floor.

Tip: If you have a cat toy with a "Use Only Under Supervision" label, store it somewhere inaccessible to your cat when you're not playing with them.

Besides the items listed above, here are more household items that could be dangerous to cats.

Electrical Cords: Some cats will chew electrical cords, which can cause several serious risks, including electrocution. If you can, it's safest to position these cords and wires somewhere your cat can't access. When that's not possible, cover the cords with electrical cord covers, foil, or double-sided tape to discourage chewing. Also, unplug any appliances that aren't in use. To keep the cat's focus away from the cords, provide them with plenty of toys.

Medications and Cleaning Products: Keep all medications and cleaning products out of your cat's reach. Remember that he or she can jump onto countertops and even get inside cabinets. Ingesting medicines or cleaning products can be fatal for cats, so be careful not to drop or spill any of these items on the floor. Clean up any spills right away and rinse the area with water.

> **Tip:** If you or someone in your home uses topical minoxidil (hair growth treatment), be diligent about handwashing after every application and immediately clean up any drips or spills. This medication is very toxic to cats, and your pet could die even from one lick. Be sure to store this product out of your cat's reach. If your cat has access to bedrooms, wash pillowcases frequently.

Kitchen Trash Container: Discarded food in the trash container might tempt a cat to dig through it. She might consume something spoiled or toxic or get injured on a sharp can lid or similar object. To avoid these dangers, either keep your trash container in a place the cat can't access or use a container with a lid she's unable to open.

Toilets: Toilets may contain cleaning products that are harmful to cats. To prevent a cat from drinking from the toilet, always keep the lid closed.

Hidden Spaces: Cats sometimes hide and nap in unexpected spots, such as the washer, dryer, dishwasher, under foldaway beds, sleeper sofas, reclining chairs, and inside drawers or cabinets. To prevent accidental injuries, always check these areas before using them. It's also a good idea to keep the doors of your washer, dryer, and dishwasher closed when they are not in use.

Foods Harmful to Cats

- Alcohol
- Avocado
- Bones in meat
- Chocolate
- Garlic
- Grapes
- Onions
- Raw meat
- Uncooked eggs
- Xylitol (a sweetener)

Tip: Avoid giving your cat milk because most cats are lactose intolerant, and milk can cause stomach issues.

House Plants and Flowers

As a cat owner, making sure the plants and flowers in your home are cat-friendly can give you peace of mind. Although cats are carnivores, many can't resist nibbling on houseplants. While some plants are harmless, others can cause symptoms like stomach upset, diarrhea, vomiting, and even kidney failure if a cat consumes a small amount. For example, plants in the lily family are toxic to cats and can be deadly without prompt treatment.

Since it's impossible to watch your cat day and night, it's critical to ensure every plant and flower in your home is cat-friendly. Here are a few simple ways to enjoy the beauty of indoor plants and flowers while keeping your feline friend safe.

Christmas Cactus is a cat-safe plant.

Search Online

Search the web for the names of plants and flowers you currently have or are considering buying. Be sure to check a few reliable sources to ensure you're getting accurate information. Remember, even some wildflowers, such as tiger lilies and daisies, can be toxic.

Avoid and Remove Potentially Toxic Plants

Avoid buying plants considered toxic to cats. If you already have them, either keep them in a room your cat can't get into or give them to someone you know who doesn't have pets. If it's a plant in the lily family or another known to be very toxic, it's best not to have those in the house at all.

. . .

Keep the Plants in Hard-to-Reach Places

To discourage a cat from chewing on your plants (even if they're non-toxic), keep them in locations or rooms your cat can't access.

Buy or Grow Cat Grass

Organic cat grass provides a safe source of greens for your cat. You can buy seeds or pre-grown containers at many pet stores and online. The grass grows quickly and helps keep cats' attention away from houseplants.

The Zebra Haworthia (succulent) is a cat-safe option for your home.

Non-Toxic Plants and Flowers

Here are a few cat-safe plants and flowers:

- African Violet
- Boston Fern
- Christmas Cactus
- Rose and Mini Rose
- Spider Plant
- Star Jasmine
- Sunflowers
- Venus Fly Trap
- Zebra Haworthia

Tip: Even if a plant or flower is non-toxic to cats, it might cause stomach upset if they consume large quantities.

Toxic Plants and Flowers

Here are a few plants and flowers to avoid if you have cats in your home:

- Aloe
- Amaryllis
- Baby's Breath
- Calla Lily
- Easter Lily
- Iris
- Kalanchoe
- Poinsettia
- Primrose
- Rhododendron

- Tiger Lily
- Yucca

Keep a Cat First Aid Kit in Your Home

If your cat is injured, consult a veterinarian immediately; however, a cat first aid kit provides various supplies for treating minor injuries until veterinary care is available. Ideally, choose a portable kit that's compact enough to bring with you in an emergency evacuation or natural disaster.

Learn More About Cat Safety

For further information about cat safety, I suggest visiting the ASPCA's Animal Poison Control website to find lists of poisonous plants, human foods to avoid feeding your cat, and household products that can be poisonous to cats.

https://www.aspca.org/pet-care/animal-poison-control

> **Safety Tip:** If your cat ever eats or drinks something harmful, immediately contact your vet or the ASPCA's 24-hour Animal Poison Control Hotline at 1-888-426-4435 (in the USA). There is a fee for this service, but if your vet isn't available, this hotline could save your cat's life. If you're outside the US, seek help from your vet or your country's pet poison control.

16
if you have a dog, introduce your pets slowly

WHEN INTRODUCING YOUR NEW CAT TO YOUR DOG, BE AWARE that your cat may not have interacted with dogs before. To make the experience less stressful for both pets, it's important to introduce them gradually. Here are some suggestions to get their relationship going in a positive direction.

- When you bring your cat home, give him a secure room of his own to adjust to his new environment for a week before introducing him to your dog.

- Before the first meeting, place a clean towel in each pet's sleeping area for a day or two, then exchange the towels so they become familiar with each other's scent.

- Once they're ready to meet, keep your dog leashed to make your cat feel safer. Watch your pets' reactions closely. It's okay if they sniff each other, but if either pet shows aggression or seems distressed, end the meeting and try again the next day.

- Short, supervised meetings will help your pets get acquainted over several days, a week, or even more. If you notice positive interactions, reinforce this behavior with treats and praise.

- Some cats and dogs will accept each other more quickly, and others will need more time and supervision before you feel comfortable leaving them alone together. Until you're sure it's safe to leave them alone, monitor their interactions and keep them in separate rooms when you're away. Cats may feel more at ease if they have a space to escape from the dog when necessary, so a cat tree or tower serves this purpose well.

Over time, there's a good chance your pets will become close friends.

17
teach children how to treat your cat

If you have young children at home, teach them to treat your cat with kindness and respect. Some children may not realize they shouldn't pull a cat's tail or engage in rough play with it. Show them how to pet the cat gently and explain the importance of giving him or her space when eating or resting.

18
keep your cat indoors

INDOOR CATS TEND TO LIVE LONGER AND HEALTHIER LIVES. CATS allowed to roam outdoors face several risks. These include exposure to diseases from other cats or wild animals, the dangers of vehicle traffic, attacks from dogs or wild animals,

AND THE POSSIBILITY OF GETTING LOST OR STOLEN. KEEPING YOUR cat indoors is the best way to ensure their safety and well-being.

As a pet parent of an indoor cat, you'll want to take the necessary steps to ensure your cat doesn't sneak outside. You can do this by keeping screens on every window and being aware of your cat's location anytime you open doors. If you have guests over, please remind them not to let your cat outside. Alternatively, keep the cat in a closed room until your guests leave.

Create a cat-friendly environment in your home by providing a window perch for your cat to see outdoors, a cat tree to climb and scratch, and enough toys to keep them entertained and active throughout the day. Cats may seem independent, but taking time to interact and play with them will build your relationship with your cat and help keep them happy and thriving.

closing

Congratulations on being a first-time cat owner! I hope you've found this guide helpful and enjoy having a feline friend in your life as much as I do.

about the author

Carolyn Kaye is a freelance writer and lifelong animal lover who has had cats much of her life. She wrote this book to share what she's learned about keeping them happy and healthy with fellow cat lovers.

www.ingramcontent.com/pod-product-compliance
Lightning Source LLC
Chambersburg PA
CBHW052131030426
42337CB00028B/5110